# Cancer Predictions and Rituals 2024

## Astrologers
## Alina A. Rubi and Angeline Rubi

*Published Independently*

*All rights reserved © 2024.*

*Astrologers: Alina A. Rubi and Angeline Rubi*

*Email: rubiediciones29@gmail.com*

*Editing: Angeline A. Rubi*

*rubiediciones29@gmail.com*

# General Predictions 2024

*The year 2024 has arrived! A significant year at the astrological level. We will witness events that will have an impact on the world in a general way, a period of collective transformation is coming. A period of reflection, abstraction, evaluation, and separation of what no longer works.*

*We will experience a restructuring of political systems, involving changes in the balance of power, manifestation of new political trends, and transformations in the way authorities and government's function.*

*Pluto's energy will cause significant changes in the economy, new industries and companies will develop, but the decline of the established ones will continue. It is the beginning of a new economic cycle with much potential for innovation.*

*Pluto will continue to exert catastrophic effects on the social structure of countries. All issues related to power, control and authority will be on the front page of the news this year. This will result in new power structures being established. It is the beginning of an era with more values and social awareness.*

*A shift in the forces of world power is coming because the return of Pluto signifies a time of metamorphosis for the United States. This implies a change in the balance of power among all the countries of the world, and we will see the emergence of new actors at the global level, and the transformation of world relations.*

*On January 20, 2024, at 7:51 p.m. (EST) Pluto transits Capricorn into Aquarius. This is not a definitive transit because Pluto will return to the sign of Capricorn near the day of the U.S. elections and will return to Aquarius on November 19, 2024. These elections will be unforgettable, as Pluto's stay in Capricorn from September 1 to November 19 coincides with these elections. This transit increases the insecurity, distrust, dilemma, and commotion of the political atmosphere.*

*During the run-up to the elections, the country will be confronted with serious and far-reaching issues of authority and democracy. The outcome of these elections will be a planetary signal of the change and evolution that is needed. It will be the voice of the issues of the transiting planet Pluto.*

*As Pluto transits into the sign of Aquarius, significant changes will begin to take place on a global level. This transit will lead to a deep and comprehensive analysis of the way authority, governments and social methods are managed around the world. All power structures will be destroyed and established norms will be challenged. All these changes will take place gradually.*

*All these astrological events will impact us on a personal level. All global changes tend to motivate us to grow as individuals. If you can understand the issues and energies at play, you will have the opportunity to prepare for changes that may directly affect you.*

*As the world undergoes these changes in societal values, our own values will be transformed. This involves re-evaluating our beliefs, priorities, and way of thinking. As our values change, we will relate to people who will share our beliefs, and this will be an opportunity to analyze our current relationships.*

*The financial changes that will result from these influences will create new opportunities at the professional level because new industries will emerge. You must stay informed about new economic trends so that you can be successful in these evolving systems.*

*Pluto's official entrance into Aquarius begins on November 19, 2024, Pluto deforms, corrupts, and transforms the themes of the planet that rules the sign through which it transits. These themes go through a process of death and rebirth, and in the end are changed forever.*

*The Aquarius sign is linked to science, scientific discoveries, technology, the cosmos, political and social revolutions, social changes, and liberal ideas.*

*The possible events of Pluto in Aquarius include a wide range of technological and scientific breakthroughs. Many specific breakthroughs in artificial intelligence, and nanotechnology will emerge. We will live an industrial revolution, let us not forget that the sign Aquarius rules technology. We will live super notable events related to space travel, the existence of extraterrestrials and implementation of technologies that will decrease our levels of dependence on oil.*

*Another change with this transit will be in the structure of power, freedom and giving a voice to the oppressed. A hurricane of political developments is coming with Pluto in Aquarius, and it is no secret to anyone that authoritarian regimes abound. The political division we have seen in the United States will accelerate further. Power struggles and the creation of new political parties will continue.*

*There will be a separation of the characteristic prototypes of power as the dominated gain more power and entitlement to justice.*

*In short, a completely unknown cycle is underway. The year 2024 is a portal to a different dimension. The three outer planets Jupiter, Saturn, Uranus, and*

*Neptune. They will work in unison to help us create a completely different reality. Uranus, Neptune, and Pluto will join forces to raise our consciousness, cementing the Aquarian Age in stone.*

*We are blessed that technology and spirituality will support us in these changes towards a completely different world where originality and personal evolution prevail, as more people awaken and disconnect from the mental oppression they have been subjected to.*

*We must be sensible and remember that for this new cycle to move forward, all obsolete structures must continue to collapse as has been happening since 2021. Saturn, that merciless master, oversees this process as it transits Pisces, and Jupiter extends its kind hand to it.*

*The Lunar Nodes on the Aries and Libra axis will continue to put an end to toxic, abusive and codependent relationships.*

*Do not forget that astrology plays a role in the alignment of events, together with human behaviors. Prudence and adaptation are decisive qualities for the opportunities and challenges of the year 2024.*

*The fusion of astrological knowledge with lived experiences will allow us to move towards a luminous future.*

*Remember that as the world changes, you can change with it. If you do not resist change, you will be able to navigate this year 2024 in good health.*

# Who is Cancer?

**Dates**: *June 22nd to July 22nd*

**Day**: *Monday*

**Color**: *White, silver*

**Element**: *Water*

**Compatibility**: *Taurus, Pisces*

**Symbol**:

**Modality**: *Cardinal*

**Polarity**: *Feminine*

**Ruling planet**: *Moon*

**House**: *4*

**Metal**: *Silver*

**Quartz**: *Moonstone, pearl, Rose Quartz,*

**Constellation**: *Cancer*

# Cancer Personality

*The emotional intelligence of Cancer is incomparable, it is an extremely empathetic sign. They have an acute intuition, that's why they are the most protective of all the zodiac, that's why they are protectors par excellence.*

*They are always attentive and available to attend to the needs of others, even if that means putting themselves second.*

*He is emotional and affectionate, and friendly and knows how to be cautious when needed. They like their home and children their home is like a nest, a refuge to go to when stress overwhelms them too much.*

*They have an excellent memory, especially for personal events and memories of their childhood that they can recall in detail. They live conditioned by their memories of the past and by their imagination of the future.*

*They are excellent providers and work best when left alone without anyone trying to help them with their work at work.*

*They treat their jobs the same way they treat their homes. They are protective of their work situation and often hold important positions. They are loyal, expect loyalty and treat their employees like family.*

*They love to receive endless flattery from others, are ambitious, easily offended and take offense in many situations where there is no reason to do so.*

*They are very good traders, they like money, to have their savings and that nobody knows how much they have. They are a little distrustful when it comes to starting a love relationship, they give a lot of thought to this situation because they are afraid of getting hurt, so they do not get carried away by their feelings or passions, as they must first make sure they are with the right person to gamble everything for everything, because they give their feelings, trust and love without reservation.*

*They are very detailed and romantic, when they have a partner, they do not allow anyone to get in the way of their relationship, not even to give them advice on how to manage it or what is best at any given moment.*

## General Cancer Horoscope

*This is a fabulous year for new beginnings, new businesses, and projects. What you start now will be the focus for the next 5 years of your life. Start this 2024 with energy, enthusiasm, and excitement.*

*It marks a year of powerful relationship between your personality and your professional life, with such interaction being of utmost importance.*

*You wish to attain a position of some notoriety, and to be admired for your personal work. Success comes to a greater or lesser extent during this year, although you may consider it insufficient due to your strong ambition.*

*In the circle in which you operate, your presence will be evident, although others will demand responsibility from you.*

*In general, this period promises professional success, and you will always find the credit and protections necessary to achieve it.*

*Your business or professional affairs will be highlighted. Relationships with people in positions of authority, as well as with your parents, are also likely to play an important role, although a serious problem may arise that you will have to resolve.*

*You should develop a certain prudence in possible conflicts in the professional or business sphere.*

*However, it is a good time to focus on your goals and improve the image you project to the outside world.*

*It is a year in which you will constantly seek new experiences, but your eagerness for action and change is likely to hide a fear of establishing lasting bonds.*

*You will find it difficult to recognize the feminine side of your nature and accept responsibility for someone else's well-being. This year you will shy away from commitments because you don't want to feel emotionally tied down.*

*Others will admire your entrepreneurial spirit and appreciate that you don't skimp on responsibility, especially when one of your risky actions doesn't work out.*

*It is a year in which you will become a fighter who does not give up easily, and, if necessary, you will go your own way alone.*

*Your emotional side will be more sensitive than usual, and you will be overflowing with tenderness towards all those around you. Especially your children (if you have them) will benefit from your special predisposition to listen to them and to be more receptive to their needs, as well as more loving and understanding.*

*Because you appreciate the beautiful side of life more than ever, you could use this disposition for creative expression, social events, and business activities. And you are likely to initiate some sentimental relationship or change your current one in form and feeling.*

*You can travel more frequently to your usual places of entertainment.*

*Also, a family member may be able to provide you with income or financial assistance.*

*As far as your health is concerned, it will be a time when you will be very exposed to colds and irritations; it would not hurt to keep an eye on your respiratory tract and kidneys.*

*During Mercury retrograde periods consider the things, or people, you want to give a second chance to rather than starting something new. If it is something new, you may have to do it in an unconventional way.*

*You will meet people who are spiritually inclined and who will shape your personality. This is a good time for your spiritual awakening.*

*If you do not have a partner, remember that opportunities do not repeat themselves. If you are interested in a person, you should approach them and tell them how you feel without thinking twice. That small act of courage will make all the difference, the beginning of a love story.*

## Love

*This can be a strong theme in 2024. Anything good you desire in love may be possible after May.*

*A planetary detox has been happening in your love life, and in your life in general. This has not been a pleasant experience. All the love experiences you have been having are of a detoxifying nature.*

*This year you will take a step forward in your love life and give new strength to your relationship. As a result, your relationship will be stronger than before, and the mutual trust between the two of you will increase.*

*During this year you will understand your partner's feelings and give importance to his or her points of view. Do not try to impose your thoughts otherwise tension may arise in your love life.*

*You may have to deal with unnecessary gossip, so you should be very discreet with your private life.*

*There will be times when you would like to break up with your partner. All of this you can control, or avoid, if you are careful about the important things in your love life.*

*Singles will have many opportunities to begin romantic relationships during the first three months of the year. During the second quarter, there will be fleeting relationships.*

*You are gradually coming to the end of a slow transformation. You must continue to take slow but steady steps forward. You must act more seriously in your relationships, and that doesn't mean you have to put aside fun.*

*You must be more committed to your relationship since you are practically leading a single life, but you enjoy the benefits of the existence of two. You need to learn to make decisions with your partner.*

*You may feel a little insecure starting in March, but it's nothing that a family getaway can't fix.*

*During full Moon periods you will take love more seriously and strive to become closer to those with whom you have a strong connection.*

*You will live some months with some uncertainty. You will start a relationship that at first will be based only on sex, however, you will become emotionally involved and confess that you are falling in love.*

*During this year your personal relationships become the focus of your attention. You need contact with people, and you will be concerned about their impression of you. It is time to examine your behavior in relation to other people, especially your partner, and contemplate possible adjustments and rectifications.*

*You may realize more than ever that you need the cooperation of others to realize your goals and that the best way to find meaning in your life, individuality and power lies in partnerships and relationships.*

*Participating in joint activities raises issues that will allow you to define more clearly who you are.*

*Your identity will be shaped and consolidated by the ups and downs and complications you encounter in trying to establish vital and sincere alliances.*

## Economy

*This year brings a lot of positive energy for the negotiations you have been working on, especially in situations where you need to discuss important issues.*

*There is a chance that you may have a new position that will allow you to showcase your talents. If you have a social media presence, be sure to keep it updated.*

*Don't waste time and plan. If you run your own business, it's time to get out of the routine.*

*If you have been out of work and looking for a job, your luck improves, especially if you have specific experience or skills.*

*You could earn a lot of money in independent businesses that could benefit you in the future. If you are self-employed, you will also see spectacular results. You will experience some difficult moments financially during the year, but they will be mild. Those who wish to exploit their talents much more will have the possibility to do so. If you don't need to make heavy expenses, don't make them, and it won't be good for you to borrow money either. You need to start saving a lot more, as this is a complicated year.*

*The art of making money consists, above all, in taking advantage of opportunities. You must put the brakes on all those senseless and unordered desires and plan a better strategy to earn money. If you do not define your goals, you will not be able to succeed.*

*You learned many lessons regarding finances during 2023. This new year, because of all that knowledge, when you must decide, you will leave impulsiveness aside and resort to patience and tolerance. All your business dealings will bring you profits.*

*You will receive proposals that will allow you to choose between different beneficial options to grow in your professional area. You should carefully analyze all the details so that your final decision is the one that will bring you the most benefits.*

*Do not allow your mistakes to accumulate without realizing it due to your excessive passivity, if this happens the situation can become critical. This is the year to wake up and act. All the decisions you need to make are within your capabilities.*

*You can change your future, given free rein to your imagination. You should begin to devise projects that can generate extra income, and a new way of working.*

*Mercury retrograde periods will impact your professional area. This can mean that, if you don't like what you do, you will make a professional change. The time when you will feel this energy the strongest is when the solar eclipse on April 8 occurs in your career sphere.*

## Cancer Health

*Remember that the most common health problem when the year begins is called stress. Having to deal with all the debt we have due to year-end expenses can be overwhelming. That's why it's important to be realistic and patient.*

*It is the perfect time for you to try things like meditation, and improve the quality of your sleep, as all of this will have many benefits for your mental health.*

*Remember to think positive and be optimistic as positive emotions improve energy flow.*

*You may suffer from allergies during this year. Do not stop making healthy changes in your diet. You should supplement your nutrition with supplements or vitamins that strengthen your immunity.*

*In general, your health problems may be related to nerves, excessive worrying and insufficient rest.*

*You may feel the need to purify your habits and become more regulated and serious. Take advantage of this year to do something for your health through sports, healthy eating, and yoga exercises.*

## Family

*This is an important area for you. In general, it shows a move to a bigger and more spacious place, or renovation of the one you have.*

*Pregnancy would not be a surprise, especially if you have been trying.*

*Your natural compassion will manifest itself through actions directed toward those in your family circle who have lost their way and need help.*

*From a more understanding place, you will try to fulfill your family role, but you will do it without judging, with a more open mind, and this will make your family members take refuge in you and seek your opinion to solve family issues.*

*Your vital energy and will in the middle of the year seem to conflict with your emotional side, and you may have the impression that circumstances are against you, as you perceive a lack of support and affection in those around you. There may even be some tense exchanges with a beloved family member. But don't worry, this will pass quickly without substantial consequences. Being patient and flexible will help you.*

## Important Dates

- **06/17 Venus enters Cancer.** *During this transit your desire for emotional security and stability increases. You may express love and affection through acts of kindness, seeking comfort in safe environments. This is a time to strengthen bonds in existing relationships and explore shared emotional experiences.*

- **06/17 Mercury enters Cancer.** *This transit indicates unexpected changes at work. You will be asked to make practical moves for your personal progress, balance your income and maintain fluidity in your personal relationships.*

*Your professional area will fluctuate with negative effects, as you will not be able to utilize opportunities to their fullest potential due to a sudden change in job location.*

- **06/20 Sun enters Cancer.**

- **07/5 New Moon in Cancer.** *New Moons are traditionally times for new beginnings. What you start can be the focus for the next 6 months of your life.*

- ***09/4 to 11/3 Mars transits into Cancer.*** *The planet Mars in your sign generally brings a lot of energy and momentum for new beginnings and projects. This can help you jump into a new project that you will be embarking on for the next 2 years of your life.*

## *Monthly Horoscopes for Cancer 2024*

## *January 2024*

*You start the year on the right foot, and you will not hesitate to convince your friends to accept your business proposals, even though some will find them unusual, but at the same time seductive. Your charm will take care of the rest.*

*January is a favorable month for initiatives focused on making changes in your family and private life. Opportunities will arise for you to evolve.*

*You will be inviting the person you like for a walk, if you are single, confessing that you are looking for an open relationship.*

*Before thinking about making more money, look for space and a change in the way you do things.*

*If you don't feel like sticking to your usual exercise routine, don't worry. The end of the month might be the perfect time to start another healthy habit.*

*There is a risk that you may be unable to tolerate situations in which all ears do not pay as much attention to you as you would like. Another problem may be the tendency to flirt with the opposite sex and have fun with unserious love games, jeopardizing an existing stable relationship.*

*The end of the month is a good time for important interviews, as your mental strength and creative energy operate in harmony and facilitate communication.*

*Also, at work you will be more effective because you have no problems to focus your forces of concentration.*

*You will probably feel more eager to talk than usual, and you will find it easier to get your point across than at other times.*

***Lucky numbers***
*3 - 7 - 14 - 27 - 31*

# February 2024

*You possess a psychic ability that only needs to be strengthened a little to become a gigantic power, sometimes you can even read other people's thoughts. This ability sometimes causes you problems, but in general it works in your favor.*

*This month the Universe tends to change things, act fast so you can take advantage of the opportunities it provides.*

*Try to be careful with the way you express yourself, it is charming, but sometimes it is also aggressive.*

*Although you are a sign that does not hesitate to pour all your energy and enthusiasm into the pursuit of your professional goals, you must be careful not to overestimate your external achievements.*

*There is no doubt that professional success is important, but it would be a mistake to give your work all the attention and relegate your family obligations to the bottom of your priority list.*

*This month is also perfect for exploring treatments that relax your body and improve your mood. A massage with essential oils can be a heavenly experience and, if you feel exhausted, it will do you good.*

*As far as your health is concerned, you should especially watch your eyes, take a little more care of your skin, and control your psychic tension.*

*In general, you will find it difficult to reach an emotional equilibrium during this month, because you tend to have extreme and compulsive reactions. You must learn to buffer your emotional compulsion through objectivity based on reasoning.*

*You should especially be careful not to become emotionally involved with people who try to win your approval with their charming ways.*

*They have probably noticed your vulnerable nature and do not hesitate to take advantage of that weakness. Appearances can be deceiving, and it is advisable to get objective opinions about any person who awakens in you the desire to initiate an intimate sentimental relationship.*

**Lucky numbers**
*3 - 10 - 19 - 20 - 28*

# *March 2024*

*Don't get too attached to dreams that may be attractive, but perhaps impossible to achieve for now. You would be wasting your energies.*

*Your partner may not want to share your youthful mood. There's something bothering her, you shouldn't ignore it. Plan to have a conversation. Sometimes your partner gets bored with your impertinent questions. You should try to think if the mistake is not coming from her side. The cause may be the uncertainty she feels in the relationship. Try to make a change.*

*You will not be in a good mood some days this month, you may feel underappreciated and that causes you anxiety. You need support, but the most important thing is that you learn to take care of yourself. You are a strong sign, and, in the end, you will be able to see what is really going on.*

*Singles need freedom in their relationships with other people for their personal development, therefore, they would not tolerate maintaining a bond that limits them too much. You will be constantly searching for the stimulating and fascinating, and this search influences the importance of your friends for you.*

*You reject normal friendship, because you desire friendly communication that allows you to forget the limitations of your daily life. With your friends you are very tolerant and open, and you are not usually possessive.*

*Your ideal is to live in such a way that your needs are met while having a beneficial effect on the world.*

*Your personal values are based on a social perspective, and you care about and are interested in the world.*

*You tend to be sympathetic and affectionate with most people, although your feelings often take on a diffuse form of love.*

**Lucky numbers**
*1 - 5 - 23 - 28 - 30*

## April 2024

*There are several problems that will affect your money sector this month. You may acquire new debts, or you may borrow money from other people to finish a business deal. Try to emphasize your diet and eliminate unhealthy foods. This is a good time to start preparing your meals at home instead of eating at a restaurant every day. If you like to exercise and socialize, you should practice a sport that allows you to do both. Don't neglect your relationships. You have wonderful people who can give you good investment advice.*

*During this month you will feel an irresistible attraction to all that is hidden, hidden and mysterious in life. Especially the feelings and emotions that circulate through the invisible undercurrents between you and your partner will mobilize your attention.*

*Intimate relationships can act as catalysts that will provoke a crisis leading to transformation and renewal. In a more mundane sense, you may have some unexpected windfall during this month.*

*An important event will give you the courage to make some decisions that involve your quality of life and that of your family, you need to think well what to do.*

**Lucky numbers**
**1 - 10 - 12 - 18 - 21**

## May 2024

*Throughout this month you are likely to develop your sense of responsibility and your ability to focus your full attention on a project without getting distracted.*

*Your main qualities in this period are precision, order, and dexterity.*

*You criticize and exaggerate yourself to the point of perfectionism. This month your mind will work in a cold and calculating way.*

*You will begin to discover new things in love, and you will be surprised by what you and your partner can do with respect to this subject, do not stop looking for ways to enrich your intimacy.*

*A person you don't know will give you valuable advice, don't let distrust cloud your judgment.*

*At work you should avoid talking about yourself or private matters, remember that this makes you respectable in front of your colleagues.*

*Your nature can become twofold during the month: on the one hand, you show idealistic tendencies, and you are attracted to the good for what is just and high, and on the other hand, you feel the need for movement, adventures, free life, and travel.*

*You can more easily establish friendships with people seduced by your enthusiasm and your communicative good humor. Your greater desire to change your environment and atmosphere makes you appreciate any change, even unfavorable, that occurs in your existence.*

*You prefer a more hectic and less comfortable life than a brighter destiny in immobility and stagnation. You will feel more cheerful, even if you must face obstacles and disappointments again and again.*

*You may experience new financial responsibilities or could earn more money. A need to travel, to find adventure, to gain some independence and mental expansion may appear. In fact, it is an excellent time to continue your studies or to set long-term goals.*

**Lucky numbers**
*16 - 17 - 25 - 26 - 35*

# June 2024

*This month discrepancies may appear in the group of friends with whom you normally share. This may be the result of gossip from someone outside the group.*

*In the middle of the month, you will feel interest in political issues, and you will show your rebellious side if someone disagrees with your opinions.*

*You must be careful not to delegate to your partner all the responsibility for the maintenance of the house. You must be able to empathize with her.*

*It is a period where you should take an inventory of your potential talents and analyze if there are any that you have left aside and that are worth exploiting.*

*You intend to celebrate a big event this month, but it is likely that you will have to postpone the celebration. This is not the time to spend on celebrations, it is better to wait for the right moment.*

*The end of the month can be seen as cursed, as you will probably receive bad news at work. You should not get discouraged, try to think positively.*

*If you have doubts about a situation that has the potential to affect you, you should inquire to see what is going on. Do not be afraid, think that many times people do not want to tell the whole truth, but there are things you need to know and for that you should ask.*

*Someone at work does something wrong and you feel like telling your superiors about it. That is not a healthy idea, the best thing to do is to talk directly to the person.*

*You should never go to sleep anxious or upset because that way stress and anxiety intoxicate your sleep and you do not rest.*

***Lucky numbers***
*11 - 17 - 18 - 23 - 24*

# July 2024

*This month you will feel a little insecure at work, and disappointments await you in your professional life. Because of your indiscipline and irresponsibility, you may have a bad time.*

*You should not consume any drug; these bad habits only cloud your vision. Do not assume escapist attitudes.*

*During this period, you will feel an inner emptiness in your life, you will have the feeling that something is missing. The solution is to look for answers in your subconscious and discover aspects that are dormant.*

*In the middle of the month, you will be caught in a conflict between your personal and professional life, and you will have to sacrifice part of your work time to solve urgent personal problems.*

*You will behave in an intellectual manner and will want to substantiate your ideas and opinions. You will take on more educational activities or pursue research that may serve this purpose.*

*It is a time when you will become familiar with a variety of techniques and points of view that will enable you to compare and judge theories, concepts, and methods based on your own personal experience.*

*You may wonder what aspects of yourself you should change if you don't have a partner and what you should do to make that person you are interested in approach you in a romantic tone. The answer is to use your sympathy and be yourself. Don't wear masks.*

**Lucky numbers**
*1 - 6 - 12 - 15 - 20*

## August 2024

*If you want to avoid conflicts this month you must learn to play by the rules. Avoid watching that person you are interested in their social networks. If he/she finds out about it, he/she won't like it.*

*To be able to relate to others you must recognize that they also have the right to express themselves freely as you do. Otherwise, coexistence will be impossible.*

*During this period, you will put more effort than usual into your work. It is a time when you will be analyzing different possibilities in your profession, and possibilities of starting a business will arise.*

*You have the strength to rise to the top. Moderate your domineering attitude, as it can cause problems in your profession. If you get carried away by your ambition to succeed, you will commit inconsiderate actions.*

*You will want to get back into the rhythm of your life. Last month you had to deal with a lot of changes, but this month you want your life to be balanced again. This month is likely to be stable if you learn to pace yourself.*

*Try to give up routine daily activities and replace them with exciting things to spice up your relationship.*

*It is also important to strengthen ties with your friends and family. Don't be too impulsive, be subtle, help more without being aggressive. Details make the difference in many relationships.*

*In your workplace, certain colleagues may try to annoy you. It is imperative that you ignore them completely, these are absurd whims.*

*Your work is the only thing you need to pay attention to, so be sure to work focused so that you can achieve success. When facing anyone, keep a positive approach.*

**Lucky numbers**
*1 - 12 - 19 - 24 - 28*

## September 2024

*This month your emotional world will be turbulent, and extremely unstable as far as your love life is concerned. You must remember that variety is not a guarantee of satisfaction. Constant change in your personal relationships can result in frustration and nervous disorders.*

*You will have the ability to keep your finances in order. Your bank accounts will look quite healthy. You have saved and will have extra money for fun.*

*It will be important to exercise, but also pay attention to your hobbies, as this will keep your mind strong and active.*

*Health will be quite good because you will feel energetic. Due to the intensity of this month, your health may suffer a little. Recreational activities will help you maintain a good physical and mental balance.*

*Your circle of friends will expand, but you will feel a superficial commitment to them.*

*It is important for you to learn that a favorable personal relationship is a two-way thing. You cannot expect the other person to do everything you want, while you maintain your absolute freedom. Moreover, if you apply such a negative attitude to your profession, the result will be catastrophic.*

*You possess a shrewd mentality and, at times, can become so astute that you are prone to deception. Your extreme sensitivity gives you the ability to guess what others are trying to do.*

*This month self-deception may arise in you because your imagination will move away from the world in which we live, which may lead you to confuse your fantasies with reality.*

*At times, you feel discouraged and lack self-confidence because you are overly sensitive and worry for no reason. Your personal relationships may deteriorate because of your propensity to live in unreality.*

*Some unforeseen expenses may appear, these will not only be unavoidable, but will put your bank account close to zero.*

*Try to control your expenses, if you don't want to have financial problems during this month you should not ask for any loan.*

*You need to plan your finances and establish a budget. Avoid any legal problems.*

**Lucky numbers**
*9 - 17 - 22 - 25 - 28*

# *October 2024*

*This month changes will make you feel overwhelmed, and you will want to change your life drastically. It is advisable that you make new approaches in your life.*

*You will try to make drastic decisions for your career and lifestyle. Be sure to use your energy correctly so that you can get the best and be successful. Your emotions can push you down the wrong path, so make sure they are in check.*

*Possible concerns about past problems. Loss or death near you.*

*You may have to pay fines.*

*The relationship you are in could end out of spite. You can avoid that if you make the right decisions. Maintain transparency in your love life by maintaining a good level of communication to avoid misunderstandings. It will be imperative that you listen to your partner if you want the relationship to last.*

*It will also be a favorable month for those who are planning to have a child.*

*If you are single, you may find potential partners.*

*The workload at the end of the month will be heavy. You should not get tense; all you need to do is work hard and you will keep everything under control.*

*At the end of the month, you will find yourself in a difficult situation in which you will have to spend money on your closest relatives. It will be a tense situation, for that reason you must remain calm.*

**Lucky numbers**
*2 - 6 - 34 - 35 - 36*

# November 2024

This month money will become your source of stress, you are ending the period of good financial health and beginning a low period. It will be a period of constant changes in your personal economy, and you will have to get rid of material things to be able to face your outstanding debts.

As if that were not enough, this month you may also experience events such as the death of a family member or close friend.

Your way of being, and your behavior will undergo a metamorphosis. Your life begins a new and different chapter because all extreme events will lead you to make extreme modifications. You may even change your residence.

Try to be perseverant with your resolutions because all these influences will lead you to change your mentality several times.

You must maintain balance and not become materialistic, leaving other values in your life aside.

Expect many twists and turns in your profession. But you will still be presented with a variety of opportunities that you can use to get out of any backlog.

*Make sure you take advantage of every professional opportunity and that your personal activities are not diversified.*

*You must take care of your mental health. Make sure you don't stress yourself out, as this could be the reason you suffer a nervous breakdown.*

*Watch your stress levels and try to be mentally strong. Exercise without pushing your limits.*

***Lucky numbers***
*3 - 4 - 12 - 18 - 28*

## *December 2024*

*If you have a partner, you will realize that your relationship needs some changes in the daily routine. Failure to do so will result in disagreements due to the limitations of a very measured life. If your lifestyle is too orderly, then there will be a danger of a breakup or separation.*

*If you don't have a partner, you will meet unusual people unexpectedly. There is a tendency this month to have passing or extravagant romances.*

*Legal matters will have unexpected changes and the outcome will be surprising. If you are involved in politics or anything related to economics, you will face defamations.*

*This month marks the end of one professional stage and the beginning of a different one. If you are an adult, it could be the year of your retirement. If you are young, the possibilities are different, it could be the culmination of your career.*

*At the end of the month all the business you start will be fruitful, but you will see the results next year.*

*Your new goals will be influenced by your family, they will be aimed at consolidating your position and greater stability.*

*Be careful with forbidden loves or secret relationships that will complicate your well-being, especially if you already have a formal partner.*

*You should try to raise your self-esteem and analyze the conditions of your present affective life so that you can cancel the inferiority complexes.*

*As the end of the year approaches, there may be some confusion about your career decisions, so stay true to yourself and continue to work consistently.*

*The planets will move into favorable positions in 2025, and it will be a good year from a professional point of view. The ambitions you have will come to success if you continue to move in the right direction.*

*If you have financial commitments, make sure you keep them so you can stay away from risks. You must try and save money.*

*The coming year 2025 predicts a lower stress load. Plan your finances and keep control over your expenses.*

***Lucky numbers***
*2 - 7 - 23 - 27 - 32*

## The Tarot Cards, an Enigmatic and Psychological World.

*The word Tarot means "royal road", it is a millenary practice, it is not known exactly who invented card games in general, nor the Tarot in particular; there are the most dissimilar hypotheses in this sense.*

*Some say that it arose in Atlantis or Egypt, but others believe that tarots came from China or India, from the ancient land of the gypsies, or that they arrived in Europe through the Cathars. The fact is that tarot cards distill astrological, alchemical, esoteric, and religious symbolism, both Christian and pagan.*

*Until recently, if you mentioned the word 'tarot' to some people, it was common for them to imagine a gypsy sitting in front of a crystal ball in a room surrounded by mysticism, or to think of black magic or witchcraft, but nowadays this has changed.*

*This ancient technique has been adapting to the new times, it has joined technology and many young people feel a deep interest in it.*

*Young people have isolated themselves from religion because they believe that they will not find the solution to what they need there, they realized the duality of this, something that does not happen with spirituality. All over the social networks you find accounts dedicated to the study and tarot readings, since everything related to esotericism is fashionable, in fact, some hierarchical decisions are made considering the tarot or astrology.*

*What is remarkable is that the predictions that are usually related to tarot are not the most sought after, the ones related to self-knowledge and spiritual counseling are the most requested.*

*The tarot is an oracle, through its drawings and colors, we stimulate our psychic sphere, the innermost part that goes beyond the natural. Many people turn to the tarot as a spiritual or psychological guide because we live in uncertain times, and this pushes us to seek answers in spirituality.*

*It is such a powerful tool that tells you concretely what is going on in your subconscious so that you can perceive it through the lens of a new wisdom.*

*Carl Gustav Jung, the famed psychologist, used the symbols of tarot cards in his psychological studies. He created the theory of archetypes, where he discovered an extensive sum of images that help in analytical psychology.*

*The use of drawings and symbols to appeal to a deeper understanding is frequently used in psychoanalysis. These allegories are part of us, corresponding to symbols of our subconscious and our mind.*

*Our unconscious has dark areas, and when we use visual techniques, we can reach different parts of it and reveal elements of our personality that we do not know. When you can decode these messages through the pictorial language of tarot, you can choose what decisions to make in life to create the destiny you really want.*

*The tarot with its symbols teaches us that a different universe exists, especially nowadays where everything is so chaotic, and a logical explanation is sought for everything.*

## The Moon, Tarot Card for Cancer 2024

*You can be deceived, lie to yourself or act fraudulently towards others.*

*This card represents separation, sudden changes, and disappointment.*

*Be careful, many things you may not know may be happening around you.*

*Use your telepathy and intuition. It indicates that you may be in a period where your emotions come to the surface more easily.*

*This card indicates dreams, the occult, the feminine part of every human being that is present at this stage.*

*The best thing you can do is to express your emotions as naturally and evenly as possible.*

*Don't be afraid of pain and enjoy joy with intensity. This card also represents secret enemies, so listen to your intuition, especially in business and love.*

*It can mean reconciliations with friends or family members from whom you have been somewhat estranged, if perhaps there was a breakup.*

*It may also symbolize that your inner emotional turmoil is being resolved.*

# Runes of the Year 2024

*Runes are a set of symbols that form an alphabet. "Rune" means secret and symbolizes the sound of one stone colliding with another. Runes are a visionary and magical method.*

*Runes are not used for exact predictions, but they are used to guide you about a future event, issue, or decision. Runes have specific symbolism for the person who wants it, and messages related to challenges in life.*

## *MANNAZ, Rune of Cancer 2024*

*This rune tells you that to understand others, you must first understand yourself. It predicts that there are changes on your path. It reminds you that, although you want to change others, you cannot, only you can transform yourself. Be true to your principles and to those around you. In this way, you will get to know yourself and you will be able to explore reality more accurately. Focus on the here and now.*

*This year 2024 demands your inner advancement. Try to change so that you can adapt to this new environment. This rune reminds you that the origin of transformation is yourself, so be ready to accept the changes of heart.*

*You are living in a somewhat nebulous period, so you must remember that the soil is fertilized first before cultivating it, in short, you must be patient.*

*Look into your subconscious, discover your weaknesses, appreciate your attributes and control how you communicate. You must be sincere and judge yourself with dignity. This rune is linked to simplicity, advising you to concentrate on your duties with respect.*

*Mannaz announces the arrival of a period of personal growth in which the starting point will be a new approach and a new way of acting and looking at problems.*

## Lucky Colors

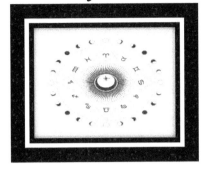

*Colors affect us psychologically; they influence our appreciation of things, opinion about something or someone, and can be used to influence our decisions.*

*Traditions to welcome the new year vary from country to country, and on the night of December 31 we take stock of all the positive and negative things we experienced in the year that is leaving. We start thinking about what to do to transform our luck in the new year ahead.*

*There are several ways to attract positive energies towards us when we receive the new year, and one of them is to wear or wear accessories of a specific color that attracts what we wish for the year to begin.*

*Colors have energetic charges that influence our lives, so it is always advisable to receive the year dressed in a color that attracts the energies of what we want to achieve.*

*For that there are colors that vibrate positively with each zodiac sign, so the recommendation is that you wear the clothes with the hue that will make you attract prosperity, health, and love in 2024. (These colors can also be used during the rest of the year for important occasions, or to enhance your days).*

*Remember that, although the most common is to wear red underwear for passion, pink for love and yellow or gold for abundance, it is never too much to include in our attire the color that most benefits our zodiac sign.*

## *Cancer*

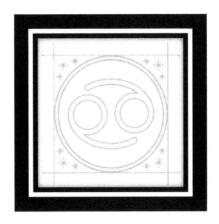

## *Red*

*The key words for red are Attraction, love, passion, desire, love.*

*Red symbolizes power. This color is related to vitality and ambition. It is also related to strength, determination, and power, and is used to attract attention.*

*Red brings confidence, courage, and an optimistic attitude towards life.*

*It has a negative aspect: it can express anger. If we are surrounded by too much red, it can influence us negatively and make us irritable, impatient, and non-conformist.*

*If you wear red you will feel confident and ready to attract attention wherever you enter. Even if you lack self-confidence, your aura will absorb the positive energy of red, and everyone will be attracted to you.*

*There is a phenomenon called the "red effect" which suggests that people who use color influence the perceptions of others.*

## Lucky charms

*Who doesn't own a lucky ring, a chain that never comes off, or an object that they wouldn't give away for anything in the world? We all attribute a special power to certain items that belong to us and that special character that they assume for us makes them magical objects.*

*For a talisman to act and influence circumstances, its bearer must have faith in it, and this will transform it into a prodigious object, able to accomplish everything that is asked of it.*

*In the everyday sense an amulet is any object that propitiates good as a preventive measure against evil, harm, disease, and witchcraft.*

*Good luck charms can help you to have a year 2024 full of blessings in your home, work, with your family, attract money and health.*

*For the amulets to work properly you should not lend them to anyone else, and you should always have them at hand.*

*Amulets have existed in all cultures and are made from elements of nature that serve as catalysts of energies that help create human desires.*

*The amulet is assigned the power to ward off evils, spells, diseases, disasters or to counteract evil wishes cast through the eyes of others.*

## Cancer Amulet

## The Ankh Egyptian Cross

*The Egyptian cross, one of the oldest and most important amulets of Ancient Egypt, signifies life and immortality.*

*A talisman that will give you strength, abundance, and protection against bad luck. It is believed that the Egyptians used it as an amulet for good health. This was an amulet used during life and carried to the grave.*

*It has magical properties and is also known as "the Egyptian key of wisdom". It has the power to help people understand all the secrets of the universe.*

*This protective amulet is a repellent of evil and negative energies.*

## Lucky Quartz

*We are all attracted to diamonds, rubies, emeralds and sapphires, obviously precious stones. Semi-precious stones such as carnelian, tiger's eye, white quartz, and lapis lazuli are also highly prized as they have been used as ornaments and symbols of power for thousands of years.*

*What many do not know is that they were valued for more than their beauty: each had a sacred significance, and their healing properties were as important as their ornamental value.*

*Crystals still have the same properties in our days, most people are familiar with the most popular ones such as amethyst, malachite and obsidian, but nowadays there are new crystals such as larimar, petalite and phenacite that have become known.*

*A crystal is a solid body with a geometrically regular shape, crystals were formed when the earth was created and have continued to metamorphose as the planet has changed, crystals are the DNA of the earth, they are miniature stores that contain the development of our planet over millions of years.*

*Some have been bent to extraordinary pressures and others grew in chambers buried deep underground, others dripped into being. Whatever form they take, their crystalline structure can absorb, conserve, focus and emit energy.*

*At the heart of the crystal is the atom, its electrons, and protons. The atom is dynamic and is composed of a series of particles that rotate around the center in constant motion, so that, although the crystal may seem motionless, it is a living molecular mass that vibrates at a certain frequency, and this is what gives energy to the crystal.*

*Gems used to be a royal and priestly prerogative, the priests of Judaism wore a plaque on their chest full of precious stones which was much more than an emblem to designate their function, as it transferred power to the wearer.*

*Men have worn stones since the stone age as they had a protective function guarding their wearers from various evils. Today's crystals have the same power, and we can select our jewelry not only according to their external attractiveness, having them near us can boost our energy (orange carnelian), clean the space around us (amber) or attract wealth (citrine).*

*Certain crystals such as smoky quartz and black tourmaline could absorb negativity, emitting a pure and clean energy.*

*Wearing a black tourmaline around the neck protects from electromagnetic emanations including that of cell phones, a citrine will not only attract wealth, but will also help you keep it, place it in the wealthy part of your home (the back left most away from the front door).*

*If you are looking for love, crystals can help you, place a rose quartz in the relationship corner of your house (the back right corner furthest away from the front door) its effect is so powerful that you may want to add an amethyst to offset the attraction.*

*You can also use rhodochrosite, love will come your way.*

*Crystals can heal and give balance, some crystals contain minerals known for their therapeutic properties, malachite has a high concentration of copper, wearing a malachite bracelet allows the body to absorb minimal amounts of copper.*

*Lapis lazuli relieves migraine, but if the headache is caused by stress, amethyst, amber or turquoise placed above the eyebrows will relieve it.*

*Quartz and minerals are jewels of mother earth, give yourself the opportunity, and connect with the magic they give off.*

# Lucky Quartz for Cancer 2024

## Onyx

A protective quartz that cleanses the aura. According to legend, this stone emerged when Venus was sleeping and Cupid cut her nails, so that they fell to the ground and these nails were transmuted into wonderful stones that were baptized Onyx.

In times of stress, it helps to make prudent decisions, and to achieve your professional goals if you use it as an amulet.

It is a powerful stone, with psychological benefits that make it an admirable choice to provide support for people suffering from anxiety. Its properties will connect you with your spiritual guides, and you will be able to see everything more clearly.

# Rituals 2024

*In this book we offer you several spells and rituals so that you can attract economic abundance to your life in the year 2024, because this will be a year of many challenges.*

*When everything is going downhill, spiritual help is timely.*

*Magic works. Most successful people, unbelievably, practice it, of course they will not tell you. They have achieved their triumphs because they have carefully performed some of the rituals, we offer you in this book.*

*If you got tired of failing in love in the last years, you have acquired the right book, because your love life will totally change when you perform the rituals we recommend.*

*Health spells and white magic rituals will help you to maintain or improve your health, but never forget that they do not replace any doctor, nor the treatments they prescribe.*

*Health spells are extremely popular in the world of magic, after love or money spells, health spells are in great demand due to their high effectiveness, although they are not easy to cast because health is a delicate subject.*

*There are infinite reasons why a ritual or spell may not work, and without realizing it, we make mistakes.*

*Ritual energy is wasted if too many people know what you are doing.*

*To achieve positive results, we must practice them at the right time.*

*These magical periods are related to astrology, and we must know them and program our rituals for these periods of time that will be the most appropriate to perform our magic.*

# *Rituals for the Month of January*

**January 2024**

| Sunday | Monday | Tuesday | Wednesday | Thursday | Friday | Saturday |
|--------|--------|---------|-----------|----------|--------|----------|
|        | 1      | 2       | 3         | 4        | 5      | 6        |
| 7      | 8      | 9       | 10        | 11<br>New Moon | 12 | 13 |
| 14     | 15     | 16      | 17        | 18       | 19     | 20       |
| 21     | 22     | 23      | 24        | 25<br>Full Moon | 26 | 27 |
| 28     | 29     | 30      | 31        |          |        |          |

*January 11, 2024, Capricorn New Moon 20°44'.*

*January 25, 2024, Full Moon      Leo5°14*

# Best money rituals

***Thursday, January 11, 2024*** *(Jupiter day). New Moon in Capricorn, a sign of stability. Good day to organize our goals, our vocations, our career, to obtain honors. To ask for a raise, to make presentations, public speaking. For spells related to work or money. Rituals related to getting promotions, relationships with superiors and achieving success.*

***Thursday, January 25, 2024*** *(Venus's day) Favorable for money spells, love, and legal matters. Rituals related to prosperity and obtaining jobs.*

## Ritual for Luck in Games of Chance

*On a lottery ticket you write the amount of money you want to win on the front of the ticket and on the back your name. Burn the ticket with a green candle. Collect the ashes in a purple paper and bury them.*

## Make Money with the Moon Cup. Full Moon

*You need:*
*- 1 crystal glass*
*- 1 large plate*

- *Fine sand*
- *Gold glitter*
- *4 cups sea salt*
- *1 malachite quartz*
- *1 cup of sea, river, or sacred water*
- *Cinnamon sticks or cinnamon powder*
- *Dried or fresh basil*
- *Fresh or dried parsley*
- *Corn kernels*
- *3 bills of current denomination*

*Place the three folded bills, cinnamon sticks, corn kernels, malachite, basil, and parsley inside the glass. Mix the glitter with the sand and add it to the glass until it is filled. Under the light of the Full Moon, place the plate with the four cups of sea salt.*

*Place the cup in the middle of the plate, surrounded by the salt. Pour the cup of sacred water on the plate, so that it moistens the salt well, leave it all night in the light of the Full Moon, and part of the day until the water vaporizes and the salt is dry again.*

*Add four or five grains of salt to the glass and pour the rest.*

*Take the cup inside your home, somewhere visible or where you keep your money.*

*Every full moon day you will spread a little of the contents of the cup in every corner of your house and sweep it up the next day.*

## Best Rituals for Love

**Friday, January 19, 2024** *(Venus Day). Appropriate for spells or rituals related to love, contracts, and partnerships.*

## Spell to Sweeten Your Loved One

*You print the full name of the person you love and yours on top of it seven times on brown paper.*

*You place this paper inside a crystal glass and put honey, cinnamon, a rose quartz, and pieces of orange peel.*

*While performing the ritual repeat in your mind: "I sweeten you and only true love reigns between us". Keep it in a dark place.*

# Ritual to Attract Love

*You need.*

*- Rose oil*

*- 1 rose quartz*

*- 1 apple*

*- 1 red rose in a small vase*

*- 1 white rose in a small vase*

*- 1 long red ribbon*

*- 1 red candle*

*For maximum effectiveness, this ritual should be performed on a Friday or Sunday at the time of the planet Venus or Jupiter.*

*You must consecrate the candle before starting the ritual with rose oil. Light the candle. Cut the apple into two pieces and place one in the red rose vase and the other in the white rose vase. Tie the red ribbon around the two vases. Leave them all night next to the candle until the candle burns out. While you perform this operation repeat in your mind: "May the person who is destined to make me happy appear in my path, I receive and accept it".*

*When the roses dry, together with the apple halves bury them in your yard or in a pot with the rose quartz.*

## To Attract an Impossible Love

*You need:*
- *1 red rose*
- *1 white rose*
- *1 red candle*
- *1 white candle*
- *3 yellow candles*
- *Glass fountain*
- *Pentacle # 4 of Venus*

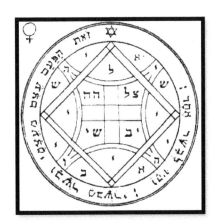

***Pentacle #4 of Venus.***

*You must place the yellow candles in the shape of a triangle. Write on the back of the Venus pentacle your wishes about love and the name of the person you want in your life, place the fountain on top of the pentacle in the middle. Light the red and white candle and put them in the fountain together with the roses. You repeat this phrase: "Universe divert towards my heart the light of (full name)'s love".*

*You repeat this three times. When the candles are extinguished, you take everything to the courtyard and bury it.*

### Best Rituals for Health

**Tuesday, January 30, 2024 (Mars Day).** *To protect yourself or recover your health.*

### Spell to Protect the Health of our Pets.

*Boil mineral water, thyme, rosemary, and mint. When it cools, place it in a spray bottle in front of a green and a golden candle.*

*When the candles are consumed you should use this spray on your pet for nine days. On the chest and back.*

## Immediate Improvement Spell

*You must get a white candle, a green candle, and a yellow candle.*

*You will consecrate them (from the base to the wick) with pine essence and place them on a table with a light blue tablecloth, in the shape of a triangle.*

*In the center, you will place a small glass container with alcohol and a small amethyst.*

*At the base of the container a piece of paper with the name of the sick person or photo with his/her full name on the back and date of birth.*

*You light the three candles and leave them burning until they are completely consumed.*

*While performing this ritual visualize the person completely healthy.*

## Slimming Spell

*You must prick your finger with a pin and put 3 drops of your blood and a spoonful of sugar on a white paper, then close the paper wrapping the blood with the sugar.*

*You place this paper in a new glass container, fill the glass halfway with your urine, leave it overnight in front of a white candle and bury it the next day.*

# *Rituals for the Month of February*

**February 2024**

| Sunday | Monday | Tuesday | Wednesday | Thursday | Friday | Saturday |
|--------|--------|---------|-----------|----------|--------|----------|
|  |  |  |  | 1 | 2 | 3 |
| 4 | 5 | 6 | 7 | 8 | 9 New Moon | 10 |
| 11 | 12 | 13 | 14 | 15 | 16 | 17 |
| 18 | 19 | 20 | 21 | 22 | 23 Full Moon | 24 |
| 25 | 26 | 27 | 28 | 29 |  |  |

*February 9, 2024, Aquarius New Moon 20°40'.*

*February 23, 2024, Full Moon Virgo 5°22'.*

# Best money rituals

*February 9, 2024 (Venus Day). In this phase we work to increase or attract anything. In this cycle we make requests for love to come, to increase the money in our accounts or our work prestige.*

## *Ritual to Increase Clientele. Gibbous Crescent Moon*

*You need:*
*- 5 rue leaves*
*- 5 verbena leaves*
*- 5 rosemary leaves*
*- 5 grains of coarse sea salt*
*- 5 coffee beans*
*- 5 grains of wheat*
*- 1 magnet stone*
*- 1 white cloth bag*
*- Red thread*
*- Red ink*
*- 1 business card*
*- 1 pot with a large green plant*
*- 4 citrine quartz*

*Place all the materials inside the white bag, except for the magnet, the card, and the citrines. Next, sew it with red thread, then print the name of the business on the outside with red ink. Leave the bag under the counter or in a drawer in your desk for a full week.*

*After this time, you bury it at the bottom of the pot with the magnet stone and the business card. Finally, place the four citrines on top of the earth of the pot in the direction of the four cardinal points.*

## Prosperity Spell

*You need:*

*- 3 pyrites or citrine quartz*

*- 3 gold coins*

*- 1 gold candle*

*- 1 red sachet*

*On the first day of the New Moon, you place a table near a window; on the table you will place the coins and the quartz in the form of a triangle. You light the candle, place it in the middle and looking at the sky you repeat three times the following prayer:*

*"Moon that illuminates my life, use the power you have to attract money to me and make these coins multiply."*

*When the candle is consumed, put the coins and quartz with the right hand in the red bag, carry it always with you, it will be your talisman to attract money, no one should touch it.*

### *Best Rituals for Love*
*February 11, 22, 25, 2024. For spells or rituals related to love, contracts, and partnerships.*

## *Ritual to Consolidate Love*

*This spell is most effective during the Full Moon phase.*

*You need:*
*- 1 wooden box*
*- Photographs*
*- Honey*
*- Red rose petals*
*- 1 amethyst quartz*
*- Cinnamon stick*

*You should take the photographs, print their full names and dates of birth, place them inside the box so that they are facing each other.*

*Add the honey, rose petals, amethyst, and cinnamon.*

*Place the box under your bed for thirteen days. After this time remove the amethyst from the box and wash it with Moon water.*

*You should keep it with you as an amulet to attract the love you long for. The rest you should take it to a river or a forest.*

### *Ritual to Rescue a Love in Decay*

*You need:*
*- 2 red candles*
*- 1 piece of yellow paper*
*- 1 red envelope*
*- 1 red pencil*
*- 1 photo of the loved one and a photo of you*
*- 1 metal container*
*- 1 red ribbon*
*- New sewing needle*

*This ritual is most effective during the Crescent Moon phase and on a Friday at the time of the planet Venus or the Sun. You should consecrate your candles with rose oil or cinnamon.*

*You write on the yellow paper with the red pencil your name and your partner's name. You also write what you wish with short but precise words. Print the names on each candle with the sewing needle. Light the candles and place the paper between the photos face to face and tie them with the ribbon. Burn the photos in the metal container with the candle that has your name on it and repeat aloud:*

*"Our is strengthened by the force of the universe and all the energies that exist throughout time".*

*Place the ashes in the envelope and when the candles are consumed, place the envelope under your mattress at the headboard.*

## Best Rituals for Health

*February 4,12,19, 2024. Advisable periods for surgical interventions since it favors the healing capacity.*

## Ritual for Health

*Boil several white rose petals, rosemary, and rue in a pot. When it cools, add rose essence and almond oil. Light five purple candles in your bathroom, which you have previously consecrated with orange and eucalyptus oil. On one candle you should print the name of the person. Take a bath with this water and while you are bathing, you must visualize that diseases will not come near you or your family.*

### Ritual for the Health in the Crescent Moon Phase

*In an aluminum foil you will place sea salt, 3 cloves of garlic, four bay leaves, five leaves of rue, a black tourmaline, and a piece of paper with the name of the person. Fold it and tie it with a purple ribbon. Carry this amulet with you in your jacket pocket or purse.*

# *Rituals for the Month of March*

## March 2024

| Sunday | Monday | Tuesday | Wednesday | Thursday | Friday | Saturday |
|---|---|---|---|---|---|---|
|  |  |  |  |  | 1 | 2 |
| 3 | 4 | 5 | 6 | 7 | 8 | 9 |
| 10 New Moon | 11 | 12 | 13 | 14 | 15 | 16 |
| 17 | 18 | 19 | 20 | 21 | 22 | 23 |
| 24 Full Moon | 25 | 26 | 27 | 28 | 29 | 30 |
| 31 |  |  |  |  |  |  |

*March 10, 2024, Pisces New Moon 20°16'.*

*March 24, 2024, Full Moon Libra 5°07' (Penumbral Lunar Eclipse 5°13')*

## *Best money rituals*

*March 8,10,22, 2024. Rituals related to prosperity and obtaining jobs.*

## *Spell for Success in Job Interviews.*

*Place in a green bag three leaves of sage, basil, parsley, and rue. Add a tiger eye quartz and a malachite.*

*Close the bag with a golden ribbon. To activate it you put it in your left hand at the level of your heart and then a few centimeters above you put your right hand, close your eyes, and imagine a white energy coming out of your right hand towards your left hand covering the bag.*

*You keep it in your wallet or pocket.*

## Ritual so that Money is always Present in your Home.

You need a white glass bottle, black beans, red beans, sunflower seeds, corn kernels, wheat kernels and a myrrh incense.

You put everything in the bottle in the same order, close it with a cork lid and pour the smoke from the incense. Then you place it as a decoration in your kitchen.

## Gypsy Spell for Prosperity

Get a medium-sized clay pot and paint it green. In the bottom put some myrrh, a coin, and a few drops of olive oil. Cover it with a layer of soil and place seeds of your favorite plant. Add cinnamon and more soil. You should keep it in the dining room of your house and water it so that it grows.

## Best rituals for love

*March 1, 17, 24, 29, 2024*

# Ritual to Away Relationship Problems

*This ritual should be practiced during the Lunar Eclipse or the Full Moon phase.*

*You need:*
*- 1 white ribbon*
*- 1 new scissors*
*- 1 red ink ballpoint pen*

*You should write on the white ribbon with the red ink the problem you are having and the name of the person. Then you cut it into seven pieces with the scissors and while doing so you repeat aloud:*

*"This is my problem. I want you to leave and never come back. Please take it away from me. That's right."*

*Place everything inside a black bag and bury it.*

## Love Bindings

*You need:*

*- Good grass*

*- Basil*

*- Full body photo of your loved one without glasses*

*- Full body photo of you without glasses*

*- 1 yellow silk handkerchief*

*- 1 wooden box*

*Place inside the box the two photographs with the name written on the back of each one.*

*Put the yellow handkerchief inside and sprinkle the basil and the good herb. Leave it exposed to the energies of the Moon.*

*The next day bury it in a place that no one knows, when you are opening the hole visualize what you want. When the Full Moon arrives, dig up the box and throw it in a river or in the sea.*

### Best Rituals for Health

*Any day but Saturday.*

### Spell against Depression

*You should take a fig with your right hand and place it in the left side of your mouth without chewing or swallowing it.*

*Then you take a grape with your left hand and place it in the right side of your mouth without chewing it. When you have both fruits in your mouth you bite them at the same time and swallow them, the fructose they emanate will give you energy and joy.*

### Recovery Spell

*Necessary Elements:*

*-1 white or pink candle*

*-Rose petals*

*-Eucalyptus oil*

*-Lemon oil*

*-Orange Oil*

*You must write with a sewing needle the name of the person who needs the spell. Consecrate the candle with the oils under the full moon, while repeating: "Earth, Air, Fire, Water bring Peace, Health, Joy, and Love to the life of (you say the name of the person)". Let the candle burn out completely. The remains can be discarded anywhere.*

# Rituals for the Month of April

## April 2024

| Sunday | Monday | Tuesday | Wednesday | Thursday | Friday | Saturday |
|--------|--------|---------|-----------|----------|--------|----------|
|        | 1      | 2       | 3         | 4        | 5      | 6        |
| 7      | 8 New Moon | 9   | 10        | 11       | 12     | 13       |
| 14     | 15     | 16      | 17        | 18       | 19     | 20       |
| 21     | 22 Full Moon | 23 | 24       | 25       | 26     | 27       |
| 28     | 29     | 30      |           |          |        |          |

*April 8, 2024, New Moon, and Total Solar Eclipse in Aries19°22      '.*

*April 22, 2024, Full Scorpio Moon 23°:48'.*

# Best money rituals

*April 8, 7, 13, 22, 2024*

## Spell Open Pathways to Abundance.

*You need:*
*- Laurel*
*- Romero*
*- 3 gold coins*
*- 1 gold candle*
*- silver candle*
*- 1 white candle*

*Perform after 24 hours of the New Moon.*

*Place the candles in the shape of a pyramid, place a coin next to each one and the laurel and rosemary leaves in the middle of this triangle. Light the candles in this order: first the silver, white and gold. Repeat this invocation: "By the power of purifying energy and infinite energy I invoke the help of all the entities that protect me to heal my economy".*

*Let the candles burn out completely and keep the coins in your wallet; these three coins cannot be spent. When the laurel and rosemary are dry, burn them and pass the smoke of this incense through your home or business.*

# Best Rituals for Love
*April 2, 13, 17, 2024*

## Moroccan Love Ties

*You need:*
*- Saliva of the other person*
*- Other person's blood*
*- Earth*
*- Rose water*
*- 1 red handkerchief*
*- Red thread*
*- 1 rose quartz*
*- 1 black tourmaline*

*Place the red handkerchief on a table. Place the earth on top of the handkerchief and on top place the saliva, the rose quartz, the black tourmaline, and the blood of the person you want to attract. Sprinkle rose water on everything and tie the handkerchief with the red thread, taking care that the components do not come off. You must bury this handkerchief.*

### *Spell to Sweeten Your Loved One*

*You print the full name of the person you love and yours on top of it seven times on a brown paper. Place this paper inside a crystal glass and add honey, cinnamon, a rose quartz, and pieces of orange peel. While you perform the ritual repeat in your mind: "I sweeten you and only true love reigns between us". Keep it in a dark place.*

# *Rituals for the Month of May*

## May 2024

| Sunday | Monday | Tuesday | Wednesday | Thursday | Friday | Saturday |
|--------|--------|---------|-----------|----------|--------|----------|
|        |        |         | 1 | 2 | 3 | 4 |
| 5 | 6 | 7 | 8 New Moon | 9 | 10 | 11 |
| 12 | 13 | 14 | 15 | 16 | 17 | 18 |
| 19 | 20 | 21 | 22 Full Moon | 23 | 24 | 25 |
| 26 | 27 | 28 | 29 | 30 | 31 | |

*May 8, 2024, Taurus New Moon 18°01'.*

*May 22, 2024, Full Moon Sagittarius 2°54'.*

*Best money rituals*

*May 6, 13, 21, 25, 2024*

## *"Money Magnet" Crescent Moon*

*You need:*

*- 1 empty wine glass*

*- 2 green candles*

*- 1 handful of white rice*

*- 12 legal tender coins*

*- 1 magnet*

*- White rice*

*You light the two candles that should be located one on each side of the wine glass. At the bottom of the glass, you put the magnet. Then you take a handful of white rice and place it in the glass. Then place the twelve coins inside the glass. When the candles are consumed to the end, place the coins in the prosperity corner of your home or business.*

## **Spell to Cleanse Negativity in your Home or Business.**

*You need:*
*- Egg shell*
*- 1 bouquet of white flowers*
*- Sacred water or Full Moon water*
*- Milk*
  *- Cinnamon Powder*
  *- New cleaning bucket*
*- New mop*

*You start by sweeping your home or business from the inside to the outside of the street repeating in your mind to let the negative out and the positive in. You mix all the ingredients in the bucket and wipe the floor from the inside to the outside of the street door.*

*You let the floor dry and sweep the flowers towards the street door, pick them up and throw them in the trash along with the bucket and mop. Do not touch anything with your hands. You should do this once a week, preferably at the time of the planet Jupiter.*

### Best Rituals for Love
*May 22 Full Moon.*

### Unbreakable Bond of Love

*You need:*

*- 1 Green ribbon*
*- 1 red marker*

*You should take the green ribbon and print your full name and the name of the person you love in red ink. Then you write the words: love, Venus, and passion three times. You tie the ribbon to the head of your bed and every night you tie a knot for nine consecutive nights. After this time, you tie the ribbon with three knots on your left arm. When it breaks you burn it and throw the ashes in the sea or in a place where the water runs.*

## Ritual so that I only Love You

*This ritual is most effective if you perform it during the phase of the waxing Gibbous Moon and on a Friday at the time of the planet Venus.*

*You need:*
*- 1 tablespoon of honey*
*- 1 Pentacle # 5 of Venus.*
*- 1 ballpoint pen with red ink*
*- 1 white candle*
*- 1 new sewing needle*

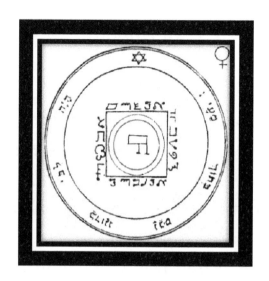

## Pentacle #5 of Venus.

*You must write on the back of the Venus pentacle with the red ink the full name of the person you love and how you want her to behave with you, you must be specific. Then wet it with the honey and roll it around the candle so that it sticks to the candle. Secure it with the sewing needle. When the candle is consumed you bury the remains and repeat aloud: "The love of (name) belongs only to me".*

## Tea to Forget a Love

*You need:*
*- 5 mint leaves*
*- 1 tablespoon of honey*
*- 3 cinnamon sticks*

*In a cup of water, you should boil all the ingredients, let it rest. Drink it thinking about all the damage this person did to you. Men should take it on Tuesday or Wednesday night before going to bed and women on Monday or Friday before going to bed.*

### Nail Ritual for Love

*You must cut your fingernails and toenails and place them in a metal pot over medium heat to toast all the residues of these nails. You take it out and grind them into powder. This powder you will give it to your partner in your drink or meal.*

.

### Best Rituals for Health
*Any day in May 2024. Except Saturdays.*

### Magic Formula for Glowing Skin

*Mix eight tablespoons of honey, eight teaspoons of olive oil, eight tablespoons of brown sugar, a grated lemon peel and four drops of lemon. When it becomes a smooth mass, apply it all over your body and massage for five minutes.*

Then you bathe and alternate between hot and chilly water.

### Spell for Cure Toothache

You must make with sea salt a five-pointed star, big because you must stand in the center of it.

On each tip you place a black candle and the symbol of the tetragrammaton (you can print the image), rosemary leaves, bay leaves, apple peels and lavender leaves.

When it is 12:00am you stand in the center, light the candles and repeat:

sanus ossa mea sunt: et labia circa dentes meos

### Symbol of the Tetragrammaton

# *Rituals for the Month of June*

## June 2024

| Sunday | Monday | Tuesday | Wednesday | Thursday | Friday | Saturday |
|---|---|---|---|---|---|---|
| | | | | | | 1 |
| 2 | 3 | 4 | 5 | 6 <br> New Moon | 7 | 8 |
| 9 | 10 | 11 | 12 | 13 | 14 | 15 |
| 16 | 17 | 18 | 19 | 20 <br> Full Moon | 21 | 22 |
| 23 | 24 | 25 | 26 | 27 | 28 | 29 |
| 30 | | | | | | |

*June 6, 2024, Gemini New Moon 16°17'.*

*June 20, 2024, Full Moon Capricorn 1°06'.*

***Best money rituals***
*6,13,20, 27 are Thursdays, Jupiter days.*

## Gypsy Prosperity Spell

.

*Get a medium-sized clay pot and paint it green. In the bottom put some myrrh, a coin, and a few drops of olive oil. Cover it with a layer of soil and place seeds of your favorite plant. Add cinnamon and more soil. You should keep it in the dining room of your house and water it so that it grows.*

### Magic Fumigation to improve your Home Economy.

*You must light three coals in a metal or clay container and add a spoonful of cinnamon, rosemary, and dried apple peels. You pass it around the house walking clockwise.*

*Then place white rose petals in a bucket of water and let it stand for three hours.*

*With this water you will clean your home.*

### *Miracle Essence to Attract Work.*

*In a dark glass bottle place 32 drops of alcohol, 20 drops of rose water, 10 drops of lavender water and some jasmine leaves.*

*You shake it several times thinking about what you want to attract.*

*You put it in a diffuser, you can use it for your home, business or as a personal perfume.*

### **Spell to Wash our Hands and Attract Money.**

*You need a clay pot, honey, and Full Moon water.*

*Wash your hands with this liquid but keep the water inside the pan.*

*Then leave the pot in front of a prosperous business or gambling casino.*

### **Best Rituals for Love**
*Any day in June 2024. Except Saturdays.*

## Ritual to Prevent Separations

*You need:*
*- 1 pot with red flowers*
*- Honey*
*- Pentacle # 1 of Venus*
*- 1 red pyramid candle*
*- Photograph of the loved one*
*- 7 yellow candles*

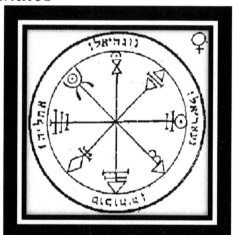

**Pentacle #1 of Venus.**

*You must light the seven yellow candles in the form of a circle. Then you write behind the pentacle of Venus the following incantation:*

*"I beg you to love me all this life, my dearest love" and the name of the other person. You bury this*

112

*pentacle in the flowerpot after folding it in five parts together with the photo. Light the red candle and pour the honey on the soil of the pot.*

*While performing this operation you repeat aloud the following incantation: "Thanks to the power of Love, we pray, for that (person's name), with a sense of true love that is mine, be preserved so that no one and no force can separate us".*

*When the candles burn out you throw the remains in the trash. You keep the pot within your reach and take care of it.*

## Erotic Spell

*You must get a red candle in the shape of a penis or vagina (depending on the sex of the person casting the spell). You print the name of the other person on it.*

*You must consecrate it with sunflower oil and cinnamon.*

*You should light it once a day, letting it burn only two centimeters.*

*When the candle is completely consumed, place the remains inside a red cloth bag together with the pentacle #4 of Mars.*

*This sachet should be kept under your mattress for fifteen days.*

*After this time, you can throw it away in the garbage.*

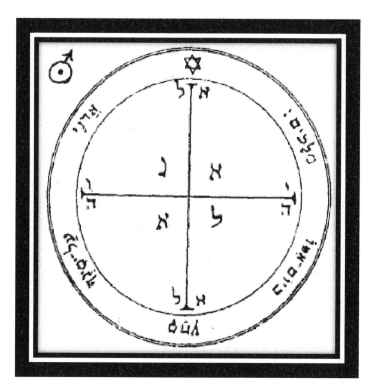

**Pentacle #4 Mars**

**Ritual with Eggs for Attraction**

*You need:*
*- 4 eggs*
*- Yellow paint*

*You must paint the four eggs yellow and write this word "he comes to me".*

*You take two eggs and break them in the front corners of the house of the person you want to attract.*

*You break another egg in front of this person's house. On the third day you throw the fourth egg in a river.*

## African Spell for Love

*You need:*
*- 1 egg*
*- 5 red candles*
*- 1 black handkerchief*
*- Pumpkin*
*- Cinnamon oil*
*- 5 sewing needles*
*- Bee honey*
*- Olive Oil*
*- 5 pieces of bread dough*
*- Guinea pepper*

*You open a hole in the pumpkin, after you have printed the full name of the person you want to attract on a piece of paper cartridge, you insert it inside the pumpkin.*

*Pierce the pumpkin with the needles repeating the name of this person. Pour the rest of the ingredients inside the pumpkin and wrap it in the black scarf. Leave the pumpkin wrapped in this way for five days in front of the red candles, one per day. On the sixth day you bury the pumpkin on the bank of a river.*

### Best Rituals for Health
*Any day in June 2024*

### Slimming Spell

*You must prick your finger with a pin and put 3 drops of your blood and a spoonful of sugar on a white paper, then close the paper wrapping the blood with the sugar.*

*You place this paper in a new, glass container, fill the glass halfway with your urine, leave it overnight in front of a white candle and bury it the next day.*

## Spell to Maintain Good Health

*Necessary elements.*

    *-1 white candle.*

    *-1 holy card of the Angel of your devotion.*

*-3   sandalwood incense.*

    *-Vegetable carbons.*

    *-Dried herbs   of eucalyptus and basil.*

*-A   handful of rice, a handful of wheat.*

    *-1 white plate or tray.*

*-8   pink rose petals.*

    *-1 perfume bottle, personal.*

    *-1 wooden box.*

*You should clean the environment by lighting the vegetable coals in a metal container. When the coals are well lit, you will place little by little the dry herbs on them and go around the room with the container, so that the negative energies are eliminated.*

*Once the incense is finished, you must open the windows so that the smoke dissipates.*

*Prepare an altar on a table covered with a white tablecloth. Place the chosen holy card on it and around it places the three incenses in the shape of a triangle. You must consecrate the white candle, then light it and place it in front of the angel together with the uncovered perfume.*

*You must be relaxed, for that you must concentrate on your breathing. Visualize your angel and thank her for all the good health you have and will always have, this gratitude must come from deep in your heart.*

*After having made the thanksgiving, you will give him as an offering the handful of rice and the handful of wheat, which you should place inside the tray or white plate.*

*Scatter over the altar all the rose petals, giving thanks again for the favors received. Once the thanksgiving is finished, leave the candle burning until it is completely consumed. The last thing to do is to gather all the remains of the candle, the incense, the rice, and the wheat, and place them in a plastic bag and throw it in a place where there are trees without the bag.*

*Place the angel stamp together with the rose petals inside the box and place it in a safe place in your home. The energized perfume, use it when you feel the energies are going down, while visualizing your angel and asking for her protection.*

# Protective Bath before a Surgical Operation

*Necessary elements:*

*- Purple Bell*

*- Coconut Water*

*- Husk*

*- Cologne 1800*

*- Always Alive*

*- Mint Leaves*

*- Rue leaves*

*- Rosemary Leaves*

*- White Candle*

*- Lavender Oil*

*Boil all the plants in the coconut water, when it cools, strain it, and add the husk, cologne, lavender oil and light the candle in the west part of your bathroom. Pour the mixture into the bath water. If you do not have a bathtub, pour it over yourself and do not dry yourself.*

# Rituals for the Month of July

## July 2024

| Sunday | Monday | Tuesday | Wednesday | Thursday | Friday | Saturday |
|---|---|---|---|---|---|---|
| | 1 | 2 | 3 | 4 | 5 | 6 New Moon |
| 7 | 8 | 9 | 10 | 11 | 12 | 13 |
| 14 | 15 | 16 | 17 | 18 | 19 | 20 Full Moon |
| 21 | 22 | 23 | 24 | 25 | 26 | 27 |
| 28 | 29 | 30 | 31 | | | |

*July 6, 2024, Cancer New Moon 14°23'.*

*July 20, 2024, Full Moon Capricorn 29°08'.*

## Best money rituals

*July 6, 20 and 22, the Sun enters Leo.*

## Cleaning to Get Customers.

*Crush ten shelled hazelnuts and a sprig of parsley in a mortar and pestle.*

*Boil two liters of Full Moon water and add the ingredients you crushed. Let it boil for 10 minutes and then strain it.*

*With this infusion you will clean the floor of your business, from the entrance door to the bottom of it.*

*You must repeat this cleansing every Monday and Thursday for a month, if possible, at the time of the planet Mercury.*

## Attracts Material Abundance. Moon in Crescent Quarter

*You need:*

*- 1 gold coin or a gold object, without stones.*

*- 1 copper coin*

- 1 silver coin

During a Crescent Moon night with the coins in your hands, go to a place where the Moon's rays illuminate them.

With your hands raised you will repeat: "Moon, help me so that my fortune always grows, and prosperity always accompanies me".

Make the coins ring inside your hands.

Then you will keep them in your wallet. You can repeat this ritual every month.

## Spell to Create an Economic Shield for your Business or work.

You need:
- 5 yellow flower petals
- Sunflower seeds
- Sun-dried lemon peel
- Wheat flour
- 3 coins of common use

Crush the yellow flowers and sunflower seeds in a mortar and pestle, then add the lemon peel and the wheat flour.

Mix the ingredients well and store them together with the three coins in a hermetically sealed jar.

*This preparation should be used every morning before leaving home.*

*You should introduce the fingertips of the five fingers of your left hand first and then of your right hand into the bottle, then rub it on the palms of your hands.*

### Best Rituals for Love

*Any day in July.*

### Express Money Spell.

*This spell is most effective if you cast it on a Thursday.*

*You are going to fill a glass bowl with rice.*

*Then you light a green candle (which you must have previously consecrated) and place it in the center of the fountain.*

*You light the cinnamon incense and circle the fountain with its smoke clockwise six times.*

*While performing this procedure, mentally repeat: "I open my mind and heart to wealth.*

*Abundance comes to me, now and all is well.*

*The universe is radiating wealth into my life, now". The leftovers you can throw away in the trash.*

## Bathroom to Attract Financial Gain

*You need:*

*- 1 rue plant*

*- Flowery water*

*- 5 yellow flowers*

*- 5 tablespoons of honey*

*- 5 cinnamon sticks*

*- 5 drops of sandalwood essence*

*- 1 stick of sandalwood incense*

*On the first day of the Crescent Moon during an hour favorable for prosperity, boil all the ingredients for five minutes, except for the Aguaflorida and the incense. Divide this bath because you must do it for five days. The one you do not use should be kept cold. Add some Aguaflorida to the preparation and light the incense. Take a bath and rinse as usual. Slowly drop the preparation from your neck to your feet. Do this for five consecutive days.*

## Best Rituals for Health

*Any day in July.*

## Spell for Chronic Pain.

*Necessary Elements:*

    *-1 golden candle*

    *-1 white candle*

    *-1 green candle*

    *-1 Black tourmaline*

    *-1 photo of yourself or personal object*

    *-1 glass of Luna water*

*-Photograph of     the person or personal object*

*Place the 3 candles in a triangle shape and in the center place the photo or personal object. Place the glass of moon water on top of the photo and pour the tourmaline inside. Then you light the candles and repeat the following incantation: "I light this candle to achieve my recovery, invoking my inner fires and the protective salamanders and undines, to transmute this pain and discomfort into healing energy of health and wellness. Repeat this prayer 3 times. When you finish the prayer, take the glass, take out the tourmaline and pour the water into a drain of the house, extinguish the candles with your fingers and keep them to repeat this spell until you fully recover. The tourmaline can be used as an amulet for health.*

## Immediate Improvement Spell

*You must get a white candle, a green candle, and a yellow candle. You will consecrate them (from the base to the wick) with pine essence and place them on a table with a light blue tablecloth, in the shape of a triangle. In the center, place a small glass container with alcohol and a small amethyst. At the base of the container a piece of paper with the name of the sick person or a photo with his/her full name on the back and date of birth. Light the three candles and leave them burning until they are completely consumed. While performing this ritual visualize the person completely healthy.*

# Rituals for the Month of August

**August 2024**

| Sunday | Monday | Tuesday | Wednesday | Thursday | Friday | Saturday |
|---|---|---|---|---|---|---|
| | | | | 1 | 2 | 3 |
| 4 New Moon | 5 | 6 | 7 | 8 | 9 | 10 |
| 11 | 12 | 13 | 14 | 15 | 16 | 17 |
| 18 Full Moon | 19 | 20 | 21 | 22 | 23 | 24 |
| 25 | 26 | 27 | 28 | 29 | 30 | 31 |

*August 4, 2024, New Moon Leo 12°33'.*

*August 18, 2024, Full Moon Aquarius 27°14'.*

## Best money rituals

*August 4,5, 2024*

### Magic Mirror for Money. Full Moon

Get a mirror 40 to 50 cm in diameter and paint the frame black. Wash the mirror with holy water and cover it with a black cloth.

On the first night of the Full Moon expose it to the Moon's rays so that you can see the entire lunar disk in the mirror. Ask the moon to consecrate this mirror to illuminate your desires.

The next Full Moon night draw with a lip crayon the money symbol 7 times ($$$$$$$).

Close your eyes and visualize yourself with all the material abundance you desire. Leave the symbols drawn until the next morning.

Then you clean the mirror until there are no traces of the paint you have used, using holy water. Put your mirror back in a place where no one will touch it.

You must recharge the energy of the mirror three times a year with Full Moons to repeat the spell.

If you do this on a planetary hour that has to do with prosperity you will be adding super energy to your intention.

## Ritual to Accelerate Sales. New Moon

*This is an effective recipe for the protection of money, the multiplication of sales in your business and the energetic healing of the place.*

*You need:*

*-1 green candle*
*-1 coin*
*- sea salt*
*-1 pinch of hot pepper*

*You should perform this ritual on a Thursday or Sunday at the time of the planet Jupiter or the Sun.*

*There should be no other persons on the business premises.*

*Light the candle and around it, in the shape of a triangle, place the coin, a handful of salt and a pinch of hot pepper.*

*It is essential that you place the pepper on the right and the handful of salt on the left. The coin should be at the top of the pyramid.*

*Stay for a few minutes in front of the candle and visualize everything you are wishing for regarding prosperity.*

*The remains can be thrown away, the coin is kept in your place of business for protection.*

### Best Rituals for Love
*Any Friday, the day of Venus.*

### Best Rituals for Love

*July 7, 14, 21, 28, 31.*

### Spell to Make Someone Think of You

*Get a small mirror that we women use for makeup and place a picture of yourself behind the mirror.*

*Then you take a photograph of the person you want to think about you and place it face down in front of the mirror (so that the two photos are facing each other with the mirror between them).*

*Wrap the mirror with a piece of red cloth and tie it with a red thread so that they are secure, and the photographs cannot move.*

*This should be placed under your bed well hidden.*

## Spell to Become a Magnet

*To have a magnetic aura and attract people, you must make a yellow bag containing the heart of a white dove and the eyes of a powdered turtle.*

*This pouch should be carried in your right pocket if you are a man.*

*Women will wear this same pouch, but inside the bra on the left side.*

## Best Rituals for Health

*August 23, the Sun enters Virgo.*

## *Ritual Bath with Bitter Herbs*

*This ritual is used when the person has been so powerfully bewitched that his or her life is in danger.*

*Necessary Elements:*
- *7 Myrtle leaves*
- *Pomegranate juice*
- *Goat milk*
- *Sea salt*
- *Sacred water*
- *Husk*
- *8 Leaves of the wall-breaking plant*

*Pour the goat's milk in a large container, add the pomegranate juice, sacred water, plants, sea salt and cascarilla.*

*Leave this preparation for three hours in front of a white candle and then pour it on your head. You should sleep like this and the next day rinse.*

# *Rituals for the Month of September*

## September 2024

| Sunday | Monday | Tuesday | Wednesday | Thursday | Friday | Saturday |
|--------|--------|---------|-----------|----------|--------|----------|
| 1 | 2 | 3<br>New Moon | 4 | 5 | 6 | 7 |
| 8 | 9 | 10 | 11 | 12 | 13 | 14 |
| 15 | 16 | 17<br>Full Moon | 18 | 19 | 20 | 21 |
| 22 | 23 | 24 | 25 | 26 | 27 | 28 |
| 29 | 30 | | | | | |

*September 3, 2024, Virgo New Moon 11°03'.*

*September 17, 2024, Full Moon, and Pisces Partial Eclipse 25°40'*

## Best money rituals

*September 3,13,20,2024*

### Ritual to Get Money in Three Days.

*Get five cinnamon sticks, a dried orange peel, a liter of Full Moon water and a silver candle. Boil the cinnamon and orange peel in the Moon water. When it cools place it in a spray bottle. Light the candle in the north part of the living room of your house and spray all the rooms with the liquid. As you do this repeat in your mind: "Spirit Guides protect my home and let me receive the money I need immediately".*

*When you finish, leave the candle burning.*

### Money with a White Elephant

*Buy a white elephant with the trunk facing up.*

*Place it facing the interior of your home or business, never in front of the doors.*

*On the first day of each month, place a bill of the lowest value in the elephant's trunk, folded in two lengthwise and repeat: "May this be doubled by 100"; then fold it again widthwise and repeat: "May this be multiplied by a thousand".*

*Unfold the bill and leave it in the elephant's trunk until the next month.*

*Repeat the ritual, changing banknotes.*

## *Lottery Winning Ritual.*

*You need:*
*- 2 green candles*
*- 12 coins (representing the twelve months of the year)*
*- 1 tangerine*
*- Cinnamon stick*
*- Petals of 2 red roses*
*-1 wide-mouth glass jar with a lid*
*-1 old lottery ticket*
*- Full Moon Water*

*In the jar place the tangerine, around it the lottery ticket, the coins, the petals, and the cinnamon, cover it with the Moon water and cover it. On the lid of the jar place the candle and light it. The next day you will replace the candle with a new one and on the third day you will uncover the container, throw away everything except the coins, which will serve as an amulet. Keep one in your wallet and leave the other eleven at home. At the end of the year, you must spend the coins.*

### Best Rituals for Love
*Any Friday in September 2024*

### Ritual to Eliminate Arguments

*You should write on a piece of paper the full names of you and your partner. You place it under a pyramid of rose quartz and repeat in your mind: "I (your name) am in peace and harmony with my partner (your partner's name), love surrounds us now and always".*

*This pyramid with the names should be kept in the love zone of your home. The bottom right corner from the front door is the zone of couples, love, marriage, or relationships.*

## Ritual to be reciprocated in love.

*For a period of five days and at the same time you should make a pyramid on the floor with red rose petals. In a green candle you print the name of the person you want to love, light it, and place it in the center of the pyramid, above the pentacle #3 of Venus.*

*You sit in front of this pyramid and repeat mentally: "I invoke all the elemental forces of the universe so that (name of the person) corresponds to my love". After this time, you can throw away the remains of the candles in the trash and burn the pentacle.*

*Pentacle # 3 Venus.*

## Best Rituals for Health

*Any day in September. Preferably Monday and Friday.*

## Healing Bath

### Necessary elements:

- *Eggplant*
- *Sage*
- *Ruda*
- *Aguardiente*
- *Husk*
- *Florida Water*
- *Rainwater*
- *Green Candle (if it is in pyramidal form, more effective)*

*This bath is more effective if you do it on a Sunday at the time of the Sun or Jupiter. Cut the eggplant into small pieces and place it in a large pot.*

*Then boil the sage and rue in the rainwater. Strain the liquid over the pieces of eggplant, add the Aguaflorida, the brandy, the cascarilla and light the candle. Pour the mixture into the water for your bath. If you do not have a bathtub, you pour it on top and you dry yourself with the air, you do not use the towel.*

138

## *Protective Bath before Surgical Operation*

### *Necessary elements:*

- *Purple Bell*
- *Coconut Water*
- *Husk*
- *Cologne 1800*
- *Always Alive*
- *Mint Leaves*
- *Rue leaves*
- *Rosemary Leaves*
- *White Candle*
- *Lavender Oil*

*This bath is most effective if you do it on a Thursday at the time of the Moon or Mars.*

*You boil all the plants in the coconut water, when it cools you strain it and add the husk, cologne, lavender oil and light the candle in the west part of your bathroom.*

*Pour the mixture into the bath water. If you do not have a bathtub, pour it over yourself and do not dry yourself.*

# Rituals for the Month of October

## October 2024

| Sunday | Monday | Tuesday | Wednesday | Thursday | Friday | Saturday |
|--------|--------|---------|-----------|----------|--------|----------|
|  |  | 1 | 2 New Moon | 3 | 4 | 5 |
| 6 | 7 | 8 | 9 | 10 | 11 | 12 |
| 13 | 14 | 15 | 16 Full Moon | 17 | 18 | 19 |
| 20 | 21 | 22 | 23 | 24 | 25 | 26 |
| 27 | 28 | 29 | 30 | 31 |  |  |

*October 2, 2024, Annular Solar Eclipse in Libra, and New Moon 10°02'.*

*October 16, 2024, Aries Full Moon 24°34*

## Best money rituals

*October 2, 17, 31, 2024.*

### Spell with Sugar and Seawater for Prosperity.

*You need:*
*- Seawater*
*- 3 tablespoons sugar*
*- 1 cobalt glass cup*

*Fill the cup with sea water and the sugar, leave it outdoors the first night of the Full Moon and remove it from the serene at 6:00 am.*

*Then you open the doors of your house and start sprinkling the sugar water from the entrance to the bottom, use a spray bottle, while you do it you must repeat in your mind: "I attract to my life all the prosperity and wealth that the universe knows I deserve, thank you, thank you, thank you".*

### La Canela

*It is used to purify the body. In certain cultures, it is believed that its power consists in helping to immortality. From a magical point of view, cinnamon is linked to the power of the moon because of its feminine tendency.*

### *Ritual to Attract Money Instantly.*

*You need:*
*- 5 cinnamon sticks*
*- 1 dried orange peel*
*- 1 liter of sacred water*
*- 1 green candle*

*Bring the cinnamon, orange peel and liter of water to a boil, then let the mixture stand until it cools. Pour the liquid into a spray bottle.*

*Light the candle in the north part of the living room of your house and sprinkle all the rooms while repeating: "Angel of Abundance I invoke your presence in this house so that nothing is lacking, and we always have more than we need".*

*When you finish, give thanks three times, and leave the candle burning.*

*You can do it on a Sunday or Thursday at the time of the planet Venus or Jupiter.*

# Best Rituals for Love

*Any day in October 2024.*


## Spell to Forget an Old Love


*You need:*
- *3 yellow pyramid-shaped candles*
- *Sea salt*
- *White vinegar*
- *Olive oil*
- *Yellow paper*
- *1 black sachet*

*This ritual is most effective if you perform it during the phase of the Waning Moon.*

*You will write in the center of the paper the name of the person you wish to get away from your life with the olive oil.*

*Then you place the candles on top of it in the shape of a pyramid.*

*While performing this operation repeat in your mind: "My guardian angel takes care of my life, this is my wish, and it will come true".*

*When the candles are consumed you will wrap all the remains in the same paper and sprinkle it with the vinegar.*

*Then place it in the black bag and throw it in a place away from your house, preferably with trees.*

## Spell to Attract your Soul Mate

*You need:*
*- Rosemary leaves*
*- Parsley leaves*
*- Basil leaves*
*- Metal container*
*- 1 red heart-shaped candle*
*- Cinnamon essential oil*
*- 1 heart drawn on red paper*
*- Alcohol*
*- Lavender oil*

*You must first consecrate the candle with the cinnamon oil, then light it and place it next to the metal container.*

*Mix in the container all the plants. Write in the paper heart all the characteristics of the person you want in your life, write the details. Pour five drops of lavender oil on the paper and place it inside the container. Sprinkle it with the alcohol and set it on fire. All the remains should be scattered on the seashore, while you do it, concentrate and ask for that person to come into your life.*

### Ritual to attract Love.

*You need.*
*- Rose oil*
*- 1 rose quartz*
*- 1 apple*
*- 1 red rose in a small vase*
*- 1 white rose on a small vase*
*- 1 long red ribbon*
*- 1 red candle*

*For maximum effectiveness, this ritual should be performed on a Friday or Sunday at the time of the planet Venus or Jupiter.*

*You must consecrate the candle before starting the ritual with rose oil. Light the candle. Cut the apple into two pieces and place one in the red rose vase and the other in the white rose vase. Tie the red ribbon around the two vases. Leave them all night next to the candle until the candle burns out. While you perform this operation repeat in your mind: "May the person who is destined to make me happy appear in my path, I receive and accept it". When the roses are dry, together with the apple halves, bury them in your yard or in a pot with the rose quartz.*

### Best Rituals for Health
*Every Sunday in October 2024*

### Ritual to Increase Vitality

*Soak an aluminum pyramid in a bucket of water for 24 hours. The next day after your regular bath, rinse yourself with this water. You can perform this ritual once a week.*

# *Rituals for the Month of November*

**November 2024**

| Sunday | Monday | Tuesday | Wednesday | Thursday | Friday | Saturday |
|---|---|---|---|---|---|---|
| | | | | | 1 New Moon | 2 |
| 3 | 4 | 5 | 6 | 7 | 8 | 9 |
| 10 | 11 | 12 | 13 | 14 | 15 Full Moon | 16 |
| 17 | 18 | 19 | 20 | 21 | 22 | 23 |
| 24 | 25 | 26 | 27 | 28 | 29 | 30 New Moon |

*November 1, 2024, Scorpio New Moon 9°34'.*

*November 15, 2024, Full Moon Taurus 24°00'.*

*November 30, 2024, Sagittarius New Moon 9°32'.*

# Best money rituals

*November 1,15,30, 2024*

## Make your Stone to Earn Money

*You need:*

*- Earth*

*- Sacred Water*

*- 7 coins of any denomination*

*- 7 pyrite stones*

*- 1 green candle*

*- 1 teaspoon cinnamon*

*- 1 teaspoon sea salt*

*- 1 teaspoon brown sugar*

*- 1 teaspoon rice*

*You must perform this ritual under the light of the full moon, i.e., outdoors.*

*Inside a container pour the water with the earth so that it becomes a thick mass. Add to the mixture the teaspoons of salt, sugar, rice and cinnamon, and place in various places, in the middle of the dough, the 7 coins and the 7 pyrites. Mix uniformly this mixture, smooth it with a spoon. Leave the container under the light of the full moon all night, and part of the next day in the sun to dry. Once dry, take it inside your house and place the lighted green candle on top of it. Do not clean this stone of the remains of wax. Place it in your kitchen, as close to a window as possible.*

### Best Rituals for Love
*Every Friday and Monday in November.*

## Magic Mirror of Love

*Get a mirror 40 to 50 cm in diameter and paint the frame black. Wash the mirror with sacred water and cover it with a black cloth. On the first night of the Full Moon, you leave it exposed to its rays so that you can see the entire lunar disk in the mirror.*

*Ask the Moon to consecrate this mirror to illuminate your desires.*

*The next night of the Full Moon you write with a lip crayon everything you desire concerning love. Specify how you want your partner to be in every way. You close your eyes and visualize yourself happy and with her. You leave the written words until the next morning.*

*Then you clean the mirror until there are no traces of the paint you have used, using holy water. Put your mirror back in a place where no one will touch it.*

*You must recharge the mirror three times a year with the energy of the Full Moons to repeat this spell. If you do this on a planetary hour that has to do with love, you will be adding a superpower to your intention.*

### Passion Enhancement Spell

*You need:*
*- 1 sheet of green paper*
*- 1 green apple*
*- Red thread*
*- 1 knife*

*This ritual must be performed on a Friday at the hour of the planet Venus.*

*You write on the green sheet of paper your partner's name and yours and draw a heart around it.*

*Cut the apple in half with the knife and place the paper between the two halves.*

*Then tie the halves with the red thread and tie 5 knots.*

*You are going to take a bite of the apple and swallow that piece.*

*At midnight you will bury the remains of the apple as close as possible to your partner's house, if you live together, you will bury it in your garden.*

### Best Rituals for Health
*Every Thursday in November 2024*

### Ritual to Eliminate a pain.

*You should lie on your back with your head facing North and place a yellow pyramid on your lower abdomen for 10 minutes, so the ailments will disappear.*

## Relaxation Ritual

*You should take a violet pyramid in your hands and then lie on your back with your eyes closed, keep your mind blank and breathe gently. At that moment you will feel that your arms, legs, and thorax become numb.*

*Afterwards you will feel them heavier, this means that you are totally relaxed, this ritual generates peace and harmony.*

## Ritual for a Healthy Old Age

*You must take a large egg and paint it gold.*

*When the paint dries you place it inside a circle that you will make with 7 candles (1 red, 1 yellow, 1 green, 1 pink, 1 blue, 1 purple, 1 white). You sit in front of the circle with your head covered by a white scarf and light the candles clockwise. Repeat the following affirmations as you light them:*

*I am becoming the best version of myself.*
*My possibilities are endless.*

*I have the freedom and power to create the life I want.*

*I choose to be kind to myself and love myself unconditionally.*

*I do what I can, and that is enough.*

*Every day is an opportunity to start over.*

*Wherever I am on my journey is where I belong.*

*Let the candles burn out.*

*Then bury the egg inside a clay pot and fill it with beach sand, leave it exposed to the light of the sun and the moon for three days and three consecutive nights.*

*You will keep this pot inside your house for three years, at the end of that time you dig up the egg, break the shell and whatever you find inside you will leave it in your house as a protective amulet.*

## Spell to Cure the Seriously Ill

*You must place in a metal container the doctor's diagnosis and a current photo of the person. Place two green candles on either side of it and light them.*

*Burn the contents of the container and while burning add the person's hair.*

*When there are only ashes, place them in a green envelope, the sick person should sleep with this envelope under his pillow for 17 days.*

# Rituals for the Month of December

**December 2024**

| Sunday | Monday | Tuesday | Wednesday | Thursday | Friday | Saturday |
|---|---|---|---|---|---|---|
| 1 | 2 | 3 | 4 | 5 | 6 | 7 |
| 8 | 9 | 10 | 11 | 12 | 13 | **Fourteen** ◯ Full Moon |
| 15 | 16 | 17 | 18 | 19 | 20 | 21 |
| 22 | 23 | 24 | 25 | 26 | 27 | 28 |
| 29 | 30 New Moon | 31 | | | | |

*December 15, 2024, Gemini Full Moon 23°52'.*

*December 30, 2024, Capricorn New Moon 9°43'.*

# Best money rituals

*December 14, 20, 30, 2024*

## Hindu Ritual to Attract Money.

*The perfect days for this ritual are Thursday or Sunday, at the time of the planet Venus, Jupiter, or the Sun.*
*You need:*
*- Rue or basil essential oil*
*- 1 gold coin*
*- 1 new purse or wallet*
*- 1 ear of wheat*
*- 5 pyrites*

*You must consecrate the golden coin by anointing it with basil or rue oil and dedicating it to Jupiter. While you are anointing it, repeat mentally:*

*"I want you to saturate this coin with your energy so that economic abundance will come into my life."*

*Then you put oil on the ear of wheat and offer it to Jupiter asking him not to lack food in your home. You take the coin together with the five pyrites and you place it in the new coin box, you must bury it in the front left side of your house. The ear of corn you will keep it in the kitchen of your house.*

### Money and Abundance for all Family Members.

*You need:*
*- 4 earthenware containers*
*- 4 pentacles #7 of Jupiter (you can print them)*

**Pentacle #7 of Jupiter.**

*- Honey*
*- 4 citrines*

*On Friday at the hour of the planet Jupiter you print the names of all the people living in your home on the back of the seventh pentacle of Jupiter.*

*Then place each piece of paper in the clay pots along with the citrines and pour honey on it. Place the pots in the four cardinal points of your home. Leave*

158

*them there for a month. At the end of this time, you throw away the honey and the pentacles, but you keep the citrines in your living room.*

### ***Best daily rituals for Love***
*Friday and Sunday December 2024*

### **Ritual to Turn a Friendship into Love**

*This ritual is most powerful if you perform it on a Tuesday at the hour of Venus.*

*You need:*

*- 1 Full-length photo of the person you love*
*- 1 small mirror*
*- 7 of your hair*
*- 7 drops of your blood*
*- 1 red pyramid candle*
*- 1 golden sachet*

*Pour the drops of your blood on the mirror, place the hair on top and wait for it to dry. Place the photograph on top of the mirror (when the blood is dry).*

*You light the candle and place it to the right of the mirror, concentrate and repeat:*

*"We are united forever by the power of my blood and the power of (name of the person you love) the love I feel for you. Friendship ends, but eternal love begins."*

*When the candle is consumed you must place it all inside the golden bag and throw it into the sea.*

### Germanic Love Spell

*This spell is most effective if you perform it during the Full Moon phase at 11:59 pm at night.*

*You need:*
*- 1 photograph of the person you love*
*- 1 photograph of you*
*- 1 White dove heart*
*- 13 sunflower petals*
*- 3 pins*
*- 1 pink candle*
*- 1 blue candle*
*- 1 new sewing needle*
*- Brown sugar*
*- Cinnamon powder*
*- 1 table*

*Place the photographs on top of the board, put the heart on top and stick the three pins in it. Surround them with the sunflower petals and place the pink candle on the left and the blue candle on the right and light them in the same order.*

*You prick your index finger of your left hand and let three drops of blood fall over your heart. While the blood is falling you repeat three times: "By the power of the blood you (name of the person) belong to me".*

*When the candles are consumed you bury everything and before closing the hole you put cinnamon powder and brown sugar.*


### Spell of Vengeance


*You need:*
*- 1 river stone*
*- Red pepper*
*- Photograph of the person who stole your love*
*- 1 pot*
*- Cemetery soil*
*- 1 black candle*


*You must write on the back of the photo the following incantation: "By the power of vengeance I promise you that you will pay me back and never hurt anyone again, you are cancelled.*

*(Name of person)".*

*Then place the photo of the person in the bottom of the pot and put the stone on top, pour the cemetery soil and red pepper, in this order.*

*You light the black candle and repeat the same incantation you wrote behind the photo. When the candle is consumed throw it in the trash and the flowerpot you leave it in a place that is a mountain.*

## Best Rituals for Health

*Any Thursday in December 2024*

### Crystalline Grill for Health

*The first step is to decide what goal you want to manifest. You will write on a piece of paper your desires in reference to your health, always in the present tense, they should not contain the word **NO**. An example would be "I have perfect health".*

## Necessary Elements.

- 1 large amethyst quartz (the focus)
- 4 Larimar
- 4 small carnelian quartz
- 6 tiger eye quartz
- 4 citrines
- 1 Geometric figure of the Flower of life
- 1 White quartz tip to activate the grid

*Flower of Life.*

This quartz should be cleaned before the ritual to purify your stones from the energies they may have absorbed before reaching your hands, sea salt is the best option. Leave them with sea salt overnight. When you take them out you can also light a palo santo and smoke them to enhance the purification process.

The geometric patterns help us to better visualize how the energies connect between the nodes; the nodes *are the decisive points in the geometry, they are the strategic positions where you will place the crystals, so that their energies interact with each other creating energetic currents of high vibrations, (as if it were a circuit) which we can divert towards our intention.*

*You will look for a quiet place because when we work with crystalline wefts we are working with universal energies.*

*You will take the stones one by one and place them in your left hand, which you will have in the form of a bowl, cover it with your right hand and repeat aloud the names of the reiki symbols: Cho Ku Rei, Sei He Ki, Hon Sha Ze Sho Nen and Dai Ko Mio, three consecutive times each.*
*You will do this to energize your stones.*

*Fold your paper and place it in the center of the net. You place the large amethyst quartz on top, this stone in the center is the focus, the others you place as in the \*example.*

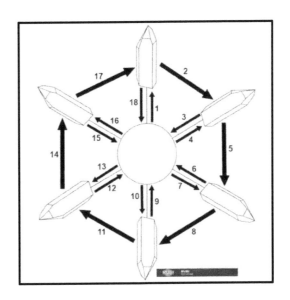

*You are going to connect them with the quartz tip, starting with the circular focus in a clockwise direction.*

*When you have set up the grill leave it in an area where no one can touch it. Every few days you should reconnect it, that is, activate it with the quartz tip, visualizing in your mind what you wrote on the paper.*

## About the Author

*In addition to her astrological knowledge, Alina A. Rubi has an abundant professional education; she holds certifications in Psychology, Hypnosis, Reiki, Bioenergetic Crystal Healing, Angelic Healing, Dream Interpretation and is a Spiritual Instructor. Rubi has knowledge of Gemology, which she uses to program stones or minerals and turn them into powerful Amulets or Talismans of protection.*

*Rubi has a practical and purposeful character, which has allowed her to have a special and integrative vision of several worlds, facilitating solutions to specific problems. Alina writes the Monthly Horoscopes for the website of the American Association of Astrologers; you can read them at www.astrologers.com. At this moment she writes a weekly column in the newspaper El Nuevo Herald on spiritual topics, published every Sunday in digital form and on Mondays in print. He also has a program and weekly Horoscope on the YouTube channel of this newspaper. Her Astrological Yearbook is published every year in the newspaper "Diario las Américas", under the column Rubi Astrologa.*

*Rubi has authored several articles on astrology for the monthly publication "Today's Astrologer", has taught classes on Astrology, Tarot, Palm Reading, Crystal Healing, and Esotericism. She has weekly videos on esoteric topics on her YouTube channel: Rubi Astrologa. She had her own Astrology show broadcasted daily through Flamingo T.V., has been interviewed by several T.V. and radio programs, and every year she publishes her "Astrological Yearbook" with the horoscope sign by sign, and other interesting mystical topics.*

*She is the author of the books "Rice and Beans for the Soul" Part I, II, and III, a compilation of esoteric articles, published in English, Spanish, French, Italian and Portuguese. "Money for All Pockets", "Love for All Hearts", "Health for All Bodies", Astrological Yearbook 2021, Horoscope 2022, Rituals and Spells for Success in 2022, and 2023 Spells and Secrets, Astrology Classes, Rituals and Charms 2024 and Chinese Horoscope 2024 all available in nine languages: English, Russian, Portuguese, Chinese, Italian, French, Spanish, Japanese and German.*

*Rubi speaks English and Spanish perfectly, combining all her talents and knowledge in her readings. She currently resides in Miami, Florida.*

*For more information you can **visit the website** www.esoterismomagia.com*

*Angeline A. Rubi is the daughter of Alina Rubi. She is the editor of all the books. She is currently studying psychology at Florida International University. She is the author of "Protein for Your Mind," a collection of metaphysical articles.*

*Since she was a child, she has been interested in metaphysical and esoteric subjects, and has practiced astrology and Kabbalah since she was four years old. She has knowledge of Tarot, Reiki, and Gemology.*

*For more information, please contact her by email:* ***rubiediciones29@gmail.com***

Milton Keynes UK
Ingram Content Group UK Ltd.
UKHW032329131223
434291UK00013B/703